DISCARDED

Aboriginal Legends of Canada

Inuit

Megan Cuthbert

Weigl

Published by Weigl Educational Publishers Limited
6325 10th Street SE
Calgary, Alberta T2H 2Z9
Website: www.weigl.ca

Copyright ©2014 Weigl Educational Publishers Limited

Library and Archives Canada Cataloguing in Publication available upon request.
Fax 403-233-7769 for the attention of the Publishing Records department.

ISBN 978-1-77071-569-1 (hardcover)
ISBN 978-1-77071-570-7 (softcover)
ISBN 978-1-77071-571-4 (multi-user ebook)

Printed in the United States of America in North Mankato, Minnesota
1 2 3 4 5 6 7 8 9 0 17 16 15 14 13

072013
WEP130613

Editor   Heather Kissock
Design Mandy Christiansen
Illustrator: Martha Jablonski-Jones

Photo Credits
Weigl acknowledges Getty Images and Alamy as its primary image suppliers for this title.

We acknowledge the financial support of the Government of Canada through the Canada Book Fund for our publishing activities.

CONTENTS

Meet the Inuit

The Inuit are a group of **Aboriginal** people who live Canada's Far North. The Inuit can be found throughout Nunavut, parts of the Northwest Territories, and the northern parts of Quebec and Labrador. They have lived in these regions for at least 1,000 years. Today, more than 45,000 Inuit live in 53 communities throughout northern Canada.

Storytelling has always been an important part of Inuit life. Even today, Inuit **elders** pass along **legends** they heard long ago. Each Inuit legend has a purpose. Some legends are told for fun. Others teach important lessons. Legends are also used to pass down the history of the Inuit to future generations. The Inuit often use music, dance, and games to tell their stories.

Stories of Creation

The Inuit have several legends that explain how Earth and its creatures were created. These creation stories tell how the land and sea were formed and how the Inuit themselves came to be. Creation stories are often used to introduce people to the beliefs of the Inuit.

Legends are passed down by many people, over hundreds of years. Every person tells a story slightly differently, so there are often many versions of a legend. The ending or lesson from the story stays the same, but some of the details of the legend can change.

The creatures of the sea are especially important to the Inuit. Animals such as fish, whales, and seals have long been used as a source of food. *The Story of Sedna* explains how animals came to live in the sea and how a girl named Sedna became the goddess of the sea.

The Inuit believe that everything has a spirit, including animals.

The Inuit have many traditions related to hunting.
Respecting the animals is key to the process.

The Story of SEDNA

A girl named Sedna lived happily with her father in the Arctic. She had many offers of marriage but refused them all. One day, a man came and proposed to Sedna, telling her he was a great hunter. Sedna married the man, and he took her away to live on an ice island. Sedna soon discovered that her husband was not a man but a raven dressed as a man. She was sad and unhappy living with the raven.

When Sedna's father learned Sedna had been tricked, he went to the island to rescue her. He brought Sedna onto his kayak, and the two headed home. The raven became angry when he discovered his wife was gone. He flew to the kayak and began flapping his wings. Large waves began to crash over the kayak, and the boat flipped over. As Sedna struggled to hold on to the kayak, her fingers began to fall off. The fingers drifted into the sea, where they became sea animals such as whales, walruses, fish, and seals. Eventually, Sedna lost all her fingers and sank to the bottom of the ocean, where she became the goddess of the sea.

Nature Stories

The Inuit have a close relationship with the **natural world**. They believe that animals have personalities and that animals interact with each other much like humans do. Many Inuit legends explain the **traits** that different animals have. Some stories describe an animal's appearance. Others discuss how they behave.

In Inuit stories, the owl is very wise, while the raven is a **trickster** who is always playing jokes on other creatures. *The Owl and the Raven* explains how the owl and the raven obtained their colouring. The story also talks about the relationship between the two birds.

The raven is featured in many Inuit stories. Even though he may play tricks, he is considered a hero to the Inuit.

The Inuit look to the owl as a source of guidance. They believe owls can help them when they need advice.

The OWL and the RAVEN

The owl and the raven were playing together one day. They became bored and decided that they would paint each other. At that time, the feathers of the owl and the raven were white. The raven started painting the owl.

The owl stood very still as the raven painted patterns on him. When the raven was finished, the owl admired his new look.

It was then the raven's turn to be painted. The owl tried to do a good job, but the raven was impatient and would not stay still. The owl ordered him to stop moving, but the raven continued to fidget. The owl became so annoyed with the raven that he poured a bowl of black paint all over him. This is how the owl and the raven came to have their colouring.

Life Lessons

While some stories are told to entertain people, the Inuit also see them as a useful way to teach life lessons to children. The Inuit have several legends that tell children how they should act and how they should treat other people. The stories also explain what happens if a person does not behave properly.

The Inuit sometimes use art to tell their legends. They carve sculptures out of stone, bone, and ivory. These sculptures tell a popular story with images and characters from the legend.

Family has always been important to the Inuit. In the past, groups of families lived and hunted together, forming a community. The Inuit did not have a leader or chief. Instead, they all worked together, sharing their supplies. Getting along was very important. Their survival counted on it. *Seal Boy* explains how important it is to treat others with kindness.

Parents begin teaching their children about Inuit culture at an early age.

Most Inuit communities are small. The people are quite close because of this.

SEAL BOY

There was a young orphan boy who lived with his grandmother. People would often pick on the boy. They would tease him and rip his clothes. At night, he would come home to his grandmother, and she would mend his clothing with sealskin. The people continued to bully the boy, and the grandmother became more and more angry. One day, she took the boy to the edge of the water. She told the young boy to climb into the water and wave to the people on shore. She knew the boy would look like a seal because of his sealskin coat, and the people would try to hunt him.

The boy swam into the water and waved to the people on shore. As the grandmother expected, the people thought he was a seal. They climbed into their boats and followed the boy farther and farther out into the open water. Suddenly, a storm came, and the boats sank. The boy returned safely to the shore.

Heroic Tales

I nuit legends often tell the stories of heroes who go on long journeys and face many dangers. These brave heroes or heroines use their skills and **intelligence** to overcome challenges. In doing so, they display traits that the Inuit value.

Kiviuq was a **shaman** and hero to the Inuit people. He was a wanderer, and there are many tales of his adventures. *Kiviuq and His Goose Wife* shows Kiviuq's **loyalty** to his family. In the past, Inuit men and women each had distinct roles within the family. The men were hunters who provided food for their family. The women prepared the food, made clothing, and took care of the children. Kiviuq's wife had a different approach to her role that others did not understand. The story shows how Kiviuq supported his wife when others did not.

In the past, hunting was key to Inuit survival. Animals provided the Inuit with food, clothing, and tools.

When the men returned from a hunt, the women would cook some of the meat immediately and dry or freeze the rest for future use.

KIVIUQ and His GOOSE WIFE

Kiviuq and his goose wife lived with their two children and Kiviuq's mother. Every day, Kiviuq hunted and brought home food for his family. Kiviuq's wife did not eat the meat. Instead, she ate grass and fed grass to the children. Kiviuq's mother became angry that her son's wife would not eat the meat he brought for her.

The wife was upset that Kiviuq's mother was angry. She began teaching her children to fly. One day while Kiviuq was out hunting, the goose wife gathered her children and flew south to the land of the birds. Kiviuq was sad when he returned to find his family gone. He went on a long journey in search of them. He finally made it to the land of the birds and found his wife and children. The family reunited and lived happily together, accepting each other's differences.

Activity

Design Your Own Bird Wings

In *The Owl and the Raven*, two birds paint each other's feathers. Follow these steps to design and make your own colourful bird wings.

You will need:

a piece of paper

coloured markers

Scissors

1. Place your hand palm down on a piece of paper. Spread your fingers, and trace the outline of your hand onto the paper. Repeat with the other hand to make two separate wings.

2. Using your coloured markers, create a design for your bird wings.

3. With an adult's help, cut the wings from the paper, and place them on display for everyone to see.

Further Research

Many books and websites provide information on Aboriginal legends. To learn more about this topic, borrow books from the library, or search the internet.

Books

Most libraries have computers that connect to a database for researching information. If you input a key word, you will be provided with a list of books in the library that contain information on that topic. Nonfiction books are arranged numerically, using their call number. Fiction books are organized alphabetically by the author's last name.

Websites

Learn more about the Inuit at www.collectionscanada. gc.ca/premierescommunautes/ jeunesse/021013-2071-e.html

To read more Inuit legends, go to www.inuitmyths.com

Key Words

Aboriginal: First Nations, Inuit, and Métis of Canada

elders: the wise people of a community

intelligence: the ability to think, learn, and understand

legends: stories that have been passed from generation to generation

loyalty: strong and lasting support

natural world: relating to things that have not been made by people

shaman: a person who communicates with the spirit world

traits: qualities or characteristics

trickster: a creature that tries to fool others

Index